Art and Soul

To Arouse, To Excite, To Inspire

ROXSANE K. TIERNAN

Contents

Acknowledgments 1

Lesson in Love 3

Feelings 5

How to be Rich 7

Spring Colors 9

Grandma 11

A Mirror of Life 13

Tokyo Winter 15

In The Fall of My Youth 17

Green 19

Brotherhood of Man 21

Think 23

Small Child 25

Nancy 27

I want 29

Purple 31

Detour 33

Life's Loom 35

To Know You 37

Journey into Life 39

Love 41

To My Higher Self 43

It's my job 45

How Would I Love Three? 47

Exploring 49

Anger 51

Celebrate 55

I Ask You 57

Me 59

Crazy Lady 61

Young Women 63

Students 65

Vacations 67

Feelings 69

Pondering 71

You 73

Control 75

This Vehicle 77

Flying 79

Eventually 81

Why We Weep 83

Parents Concern 85

Marriages 87

You Can 89

The Rubble 91

The Eternal Plan 93

Let Go 95

Tensions 97

Stopped 99

Why? 101

Bubble Wrap 101

The Rebel 103

Keep Trying 105

Fireflies 107

Courage 109

At Our Cabana 111

About the Author 116

Acknowledgments

There are hundreds of people I should thank for helping me learn life's lessons adding to the tapestry of my life—my siblings, my parents, my partners, my children, my students, my friends, fellow authors and artists. This book was compiled with help from Paul Hagarty and Alisha Johnson at Christian Faith Publishing, Bonnie Davies, Suzanne Darnell, Bill Spagnut, Jeysoca Kardell, Yvette Cuthbert, Marcia Dheilly- Sturrock and Nancy Dheilly. We hope you reflect the beauty in the Art Work and life's fullness in the poetry.

Carpe Diem,

Roxsane

Coquitlam River Morn

Lesson in Love

Learn well this lesson in love
Love is a two-sided affair
Viable only when shared
Sharing the joys and sharing the sorrows
Increasing one's awareness of the
effect the world has on others.
Learn well this lesson in love
Learn to talk, talk, talk and listen, listen, listen
Hear the hurt, the impatience, and the joy
Understand the gentleness, the
compassion, the striving.
Learn well this lesson in love
Learn to encourage-reaching out
Exploring all possible areas of growth
For when something stops growing
It begins to die.
Learn well this lesson in love
Live life to its fullest
Bring home the joy of newfound friends
Of accomplishments, of creation.
Learn to stretch, to reach, to be free.
Learn well this lesson in love Learn to risk, to wonder, to
admire To keep the world fresh at your door To enjoy the
cold and the rain of life Because it makes the sunshine more.
Learn well this lesson in love
LOVE TO LIVE
Learn well this lesson in love
Learn that love is two-sided
Love needs batting back and forth.
It needs polishing, rearranging, and refurbishing. It can tear
you down or build you up. It requires a constant effort.
Learn well this lesson in love Learn that love has its costs
The more you invest the more you get back. Learn to see the
love in tasks performed for you
The thoughtfulness, the time, the love.

Silent Sentinels

Feelings

I've bottled them up.
I've sealed them in stone.
I don't want my feelings
Let loose on their own.

One Fine Day

How to be Rich

And this is the way to be rich
To value each minute of every day
To experience the pleasures along the way
A single flower, a cloudy sky,
a trio of ducks floating by
To let your heart be taken by storm
To feel the sun's warmth on a wintery morn
To admire the curved branches against the snow
To let your heart go, to let it go
To bask in the glow of a warm hearted greeting
To thoroughly enjoy every chance meeting
To hear the music and quicken your pace
To dance for the joy of it all by yourself
To feel happily tired after working hard
To see the care in a well-kept yard
To understand people far and near
To work for a world free from fear
Yes, this is the way to be rich

Tulip Time

Spring Colors

The fluted mauve flowers of the jacaranda tree
Stand out against the sky pleasuring me.
The scent of llamaradas, orange
flame flowers on the vine
Make one remember the beautiful
and the sublime.
Bright red poinsettias on bushes six feet high,
Doubles and triples astound the passers-by.
Hibiscus flowers lining all the walks,
The yellow, pink, and salmon
ones make visitors talk.
The bougainvillea spilling over the garden wall
Magenta, cochineal and sandy
peach tumble and sprawl.
These are the flowers of Mexico I love most of all.

Waltz of the Flowers

Grandma

Grandma, do you remember?
Yes, I have a son, John.
He lives on the coast somewhere
I haven't seen him for years.
Grandma, where is your trunk?
Oh, yes, I brought you many presents...
The pillow ticking is for you.
I wonder when I will get to John's house...
I have his violin and the china, too.
Grandma, where are you going?
I must see John. I really must.
Can you help me pack?
I need to go. he will be looking for me
Grandma, Dad wants you to stay.
But she was gone.
Gone to search for John-
That other John she could only remember

Wish You Were Here

A Mirror of Life

Consider yourself a mirror of life
You are
You reflect the pain and the joy
Of those you care about.
You distort the feelings that hit
Your imperfect surface
Causing defects to be magnified,
Joys shrunk.
The less perfect the mirror
The greater the distortion.
Remember the bent mirrors
In the haunted house.
How easy it is for a twisted personality
To see mainly the sadness
The rain of life
Never reflecting the warmth of the sun.
Don't keep your mirror in the dark
Mirrors don't have light.
They only reflect.
Put your mirror where endless light variations
Are possible
Give your life the depth, the texture
Of maximum exposure.
Then, and only then, can we see life as it is-
Complex and varied.
Remember, you are a mirror of life.
If you are always with sad, narrow people
You will be sadder.
If you are only around the circus
Your reflections will be bizarre.
But think of the wonder, the joy
If you reflect love, magnify peace
So that others, many others
Can reflect and reflect
These joys endlessly.
Remember we are all mirrors of life.

Winter Stream

Tokyo Winter

It was the cold…
Rubbing against her face
Making the nose snuffly,
the eyes water and vision blur.
It was the cold
that made her lean forward
into the wind
and the fingers to tighten on the
string bag handles.
And then…the wind died
letting the sun's warmth through
letting her straighten, relax
only to be caught by the next gust.
It was the cold
The friction of the wind against the skin.
The blood rushing to the surface,
The burning cold, the unyielding body
shutting out all forms of cold
that Tokyo winter.

Conjunction

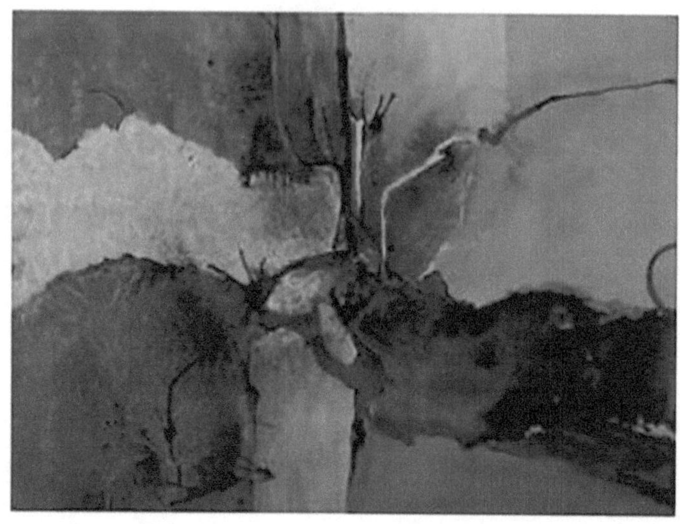

In The Fall of My Youth

She was a rebel
She loved to argue
Enchanting some
Entertaining others
And frustrating those close to her.
She loved to talk, to debate, to explore
All avenues of life.
She enjoyed the parry and thrust
The respect, the logic, the challenge.
She would question, probe-
Looking for reasons, for understanding,
for acceptance.
She needed the attention, the respect, the power.
She loved the freedom, the lack of
jealousy, of incrimination.
It was great to be young,
To sit at the back of the bus
And argue with those old men.
She fascinated them and they looked forward
To the weekly encounters-
Anticipating, waiting, hoping,
Needing the exchange as much as she did.
More color was added to their lives
Another perspective, dimension, focal point.
Forty minutes of life,
A small adventure...
That began and ended at the bus stop,
In the fall of my youth.

Come by Chance

Green

Green grass growing by the green fence
Green gingham dress, clean and crisp.
Green salads-fresh, full of crunch.
Green-go. Go, live, get on with it.
Green frog, flopping, hopping, green.
Green trees, giving shade, love.
Green moss, carpet soft, comforting,
GREEN.

Song for the Mountains

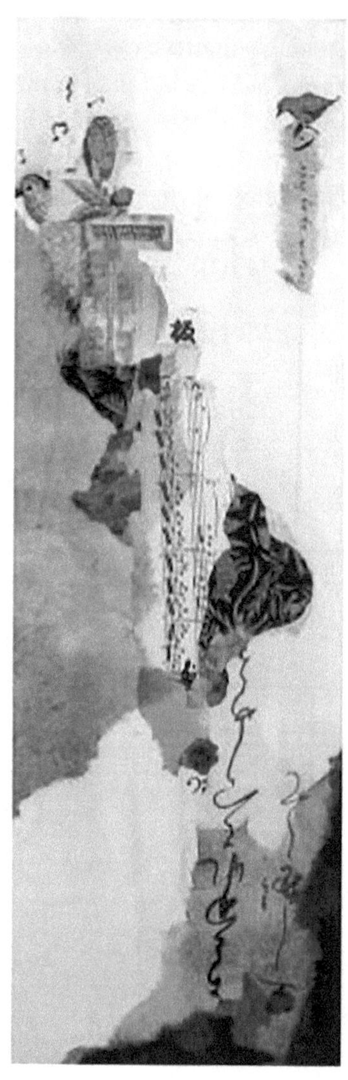

Brotherhood of Man

You can live your own life
So live it very well.
You don't know whose life you'll influence-
You really cannot tell.
You can only do your own job.
It is really up to you
much as you think you understand You
can't walk in another's shoes.
So, try to be accepting
Take joy in what people are,
Try positive reinforcement
To brighten another's star.
Try to see the whole picture
the grand, eternal plan— Remember to
add your sparkle
To the brotherhood of man.

Near Moraine Lake

Think

Think peace
Transmit love.
Gain Knowledge
Spread understanding
Feel compassion
Provide support Think peace
Forge equality.

Cherry Blossom Time

Small Child

Full of promise, Full of hope
With lots of encouragement
With Life's trials you'll cope
You need to learn
From cause and effect
The flow of nature, a wide scope
Teaches personal respect,
not to sit around and mope.
To solve your own problems
To learn from your mistakes
To always be encouraged to do your personal best
To never rub it in when you've failed a test.
To learn to live with failure,
To accept and then go on.
Living with success
Can make you very, very strong.
To be strong, to be whole-
To reach many a new goal
To be open to the possibilities of life.
This I wish you, Small child.

Weeds and Seeds

Nancy

On that frosty October morn
Two minutes before Nancy was born
"I'm sure it's a boy," the doctor said
But Nancy was there instead
And since that day when Nancy came
Things have never been the same
Her hair's not red, not quite-
Her eyes are blue, sparkling bright.
At seven o'clock, my slippers she brings
As if to say, "Get up, you lazy thing."
She's happy as a lark all day
And loves to play, play, play.
Most of the toys have lost their charms,
Off the duck's head, the doll's arms.
My china is diminishing fast.
I wonder how long this stage will last.
She climbs into the bathroom sink
And chews a bar of soap that's pink.
Into her hair she is combing milk—
Only yesterday it was soft as silk.
Quickly, when everything seems amiss
She turns up her face to offer a kiss.
Now she's on the kitchen table
She makes this house look like a stable
Sometimes I wonder, I must admit—
How I'll ever make a lady out of "it".

Evening in Provence

I want...

To visit Guatemala, Costa Rica and Peru
To maybe see Colombia, Ecuador and Chile, too.
Then off to tour Europe
the castles, the country, the people, the places.
The joy of seeing old friends
And meeting new faces.
I want to have my own school—
An inter-cultural institute,
Where more than just language Is in hot pursuit.
I want to remodel my house-
The kitchen and bath
To make the garden more like a country path. Maybe
I'd like to learn to sail-
I'm not sure to what avail.
I'd like to explore parts of Africa, too Burkina Faso,
Ivory Coast-even Chad. Sangam, India and Burma
Might not be too bad.
I've got a strong case of Gypsy
I want to go, to do, and to see.
People and places all over this world fascinate me.
I want to learn the powers of negotiation
To make stronger people, countries and nations.
I want to write books-on child
care, on understanding
On struggling with life.
Maybe on why every person needs a VERY good wife
Now that would be fun— Tongue-in-cheek, not so
meek
What else is there I want to seek?
There are lots of things to see, to do, to try—
I really don't want life to pass me by.

Emergence

Purple

I have my bug-eye sunglasses
With mauve, metallic frames
I have my purple boots
For aerobics not the rain
Yes, purple is my color
I could write a similar book
But purple as I use it
Is like a fishing hook
It catches your attention
It keeps me current, alert
The communication lines are open
I don't know what the wavelength is
I do know that it works.
There is no generation gap
There's not much they could do
To get me in a flap
The purple boots and glasses
They really set the pace—
They help me set the challenge
For all of us to face.

Wetlands

Detour

I bet you've never been on a bus
That travelled thus
Off the main road
Through a dinky little town
Through someone's courtyard
Down the narrow lane
Out through two huge mud holes
To a decent road again.
We often saw the highway Clogged, so full of cars
Then stands along our smaller road
Selling licuado out of jars This strangely pleasant byway Gave
us a glimpse of rural life. The detour was quite refreshing
We really didn't mind.
You never knew around what corner
Something fascinating you'd find.
And if when life affords it we detour
Down the track
We often find our perspective changed
When we venture back.
The places we never get to,
The things we never see
Give life a different flavor.
These little intermissions we
really should SAVOR!

Heriot Bay

Life's Loom

What are you working on
On Life's Loom?
Are the colors full of joy,
Sobriety or gloom?
What is the design?
Do you have a precise cartoon?
Are the color changes planned?
Does it suit your "room"?
What have you interwoven
With your carefully chosen threads?
Life needs a resilient fabric
Nothing inflexible or harsh.
You need suppleness and flexibility
Yard after yard.
Perhaps you began with tabby
For life was really black or white
And you needed twill for strength,
Durability is a real delight.
Later on you needed warmth
With interwoven spaces
Double cloth, career and home life
Lead to varied paces, varied faces.
The lace weaves came last
The possibilities are vast
They filter in harmony of light, of peace
So at last the work on our loom can cease.

By the Brunette

To Know You

I'd like to know you better
To understand you well
But I'm never sure who's ready
For the things I have to tell.
There's things you want to hear
And things I'd like to say
But the fact they're not the same
May frighten you away.
At times my soul is tormented
At times it's very free.
Are there similar realities
For both you and me?
How have you coped with the dilemmas
But I'm never sure who's ready
For the things I have to tell.
There's things you want to hear
And things I'd like to say
But the fact they're not the same
May frighten you away.
At times my soul is tormented
At times it's very free.
Are there similar realities
For both you and me?
How have you coped with the dilemmas
Of your own private life?
How do you handle the stress? The strife?
What are your real loves?
What brings you peace?
Where do you find pleasure?
Where release?
Are you complimentary to my nature?
Supplementary or incongruent?
You speak a language in which
I'm not very fluent.

Alouette River

Journey into Life

In the journey into life we take
Each one starts from a different place.
Each one has his own destination
Each one gets off at a specific station.
And as we travel, our plans may change
There are many options in our lives to arrange.
Some of us travel quickly over by jet
But many of us are not ready for that yet.
Some of us crawl pathetically slow.
We poke and we poke-everywhere we go.
The worlds that we see are never the same
Some seek beauty, others fame.
Some are actively involved, others only look.
Each one of us could write quite a different book
Welcome to my world.

Song for Spring

Love

Love for the blood to rush
Straight through your veins
For your head just to swirl
To be almost insane
For the joy to carry you up,
Up, up to the clouds
For the feeling you want to laugh
Or to cry right out loud.
Love for its sadness Its temporary madness
For the merry-go-round
You are on.
For the secret delight
When your heart is in flight
When the love that you share
Seems too strong to bear
And the glow that you feel
Seems too great to be real
For the heady emotions
That sweep like a flood to the oceans.
Love when the pain that you feel
At another's small sorrows
Makes you want to take them away
For a hundred tomorrows.
All the wrenching, the tearing-
It certainly is wearing. Love-
How long can it last?
When will this feeling be past?
What did I do to deserve it?
And for goodness' sake—
How can I preserve it?

Moon out of Africa

To My Higher Self

What are you doing in the corner?
What are you doing hiding away?
What are you doing in the background?
Get out in front, show me the way!
Why do you stand there in the shadows?
Why are you quiet, meek, and mild?
Why don't you push me down the right path?
Why do you act like a subdued child?
Is it because I am so busy,
Because I never really listen well?
Is it because I do my own thing
And rarely sit and rest for a spell?
Maybe I should take life more slowly-
Maybe I should take the scenic route.
I've always been very curious
I need to know just everything, to boot.
I really want to know what is the right way.
I need to find it on my own.
Can you tell me for which sins in which lifetime
This time I must atone?

The Grove

It's my job….

To question, to probe, to challenge, to create
To make a world free from hate
To comfort, to strengthen, to respect old and new
To make friends of many, not just a few,
To study the world, its many faces,
To find the familiar in foreign places,
To enjoy life to its very hilt,
To live a life free from guilt.
To be a symbol of courage, of hope
To never, no, never sit around and mope,
To consider the future, to remember the past,
To believe we can find peace, at last, at last.
To set a goal, to follow it through
And every day to learn something new.
THAT'S my job.

Letters in the Sand

How Would I Love Three?

I'd love thee with the joy of
watching a fancy parade.
A parade of experiences that's not easily made
But without the fanfare heard by the crowd
With the Mozart-like music that is never too loud.
I'd love thee with kindness, with
gentleness, with hope
With a joy in day-to-day living
that never lets you mope.
Spilling patience,
encouragement
on tremulous fears
Being so crazily happy that you
fight back the tears
With unspoken words over distances great
With music and laughter from a previous fate
Still, deep emotions that grab you again
The tugging, the twisting, the innocent pain.
Those feelings, all those feelings,
they are on the loose again
How lucky, how curious, how puzzling the mood
The acceptance, the understanding...
a shyness-so coy
Can all of this be a response to a middle-aged boy?
Oh, oh crazy love-it happens all the time
That crazy love of mine
Oh, crazy love

Onward and Upward

Exploring

Follow the confusing streets of my mind
Down torturous unnamed walkways
Through busy thoroughfares
Taking some crossroads
Missing others
Searching for life, its meaning
Its goals
Out with the busy throngs
Streets teeming with life
Leading to work, to play, to home.
Foreign streets, leading nowhere-
Lost, confused, full of fear
Curiosity leading forward
To finally find a friend.

Warm

Anger

Suppressed anger,
Slow-cooking, dormant-It lies waiting.
Just waiting for a chance word,
An inflection in another's voice
And out it comes-
Out of all proportion to the event

Tranquility

Tranquility

Patterns

Celebrate

Seeing the joy in all creation
Seeing the challenges facing the nation
Seeing the hardships,
the weary, the worn, the beaten
Seeing life take its toll
Seeing success, friendship and love
For all creation
The strong, the weak, the shy, the bold.
Accepting life and carrying on.
Trying to teach people to be positive, strong
Celebrating accomplishments.
Enjoying life!
We have to work to end the strife
And find a way to celebrate life.

Meiji Morning

I Ask You

Did you say I could travel?
Well, when can we leave?
What kind of adventure
Do you have up your sleeve?

Rushing Waters

Me

I've always been excited
Nervous, shy, afraid.
I don't know why I'm like that—
Guess it's how I'm made.
I've always been curious
I want to go here and I want to go there.
I ask a lot of questions
At times, that's rather hard to bear.
I want to do this
And I want to do that.
I search and I search
For a solution that's pat.
I travel down the main road
I travel down the byway.
There are many detours on my life's highway.
I've learned a lot of useful things
Useless things and more.
You never know what will come to the fore.
A life of exploration is for sure in store.
My brain works when I'm sleeping-
Sometimes when I'm awake-
You never know which direction
My thoughts will take.

Bab's Bouquet

Crazy Lady

Weird person, crazy lady
Self-effacing fool
Who am I? What am I?
A drone in the common pool?
Where do I come from?
What do I mean?
Can I contribute to the world scene?
Let it go, let it all show
Cry a lot, sigh a lot...
Open your heart to the world
No one can read a banner
Until it is fully unfurled.

Motoko's Friends

Young Women

Young women
Special young women
From all over the world
Searching for the way
Not any way
But the best way
To develop economic potential,
To use money, resources and people well.
To establish human rights,
To assert them, maintain them
And find PEACE.
Peace which is more,
More than an absence of conflict-
Peace through equality, self-development
And love.
Critical, critical, analytical
I bend, explore
Beseech, implore
What makes my world go 'round?
Life is full of wonder-
The sun, the cold, the birds, the trees-
A child fascinated by a bug in the weeds.

From Zanzibar

Students

Students, easily embarrassed, searching,
Longing to know, to understand.
Eager to share their food, their traditions,
With touching gifts, symbols of
friendship and caring.
Careful progress, repetition and patience—
With difficult sounds, the tape recorder and me
Full of kindness, immeasurable kindness-
Love of life and of learning
Students of English, of life and the World.

Blue Lagoon

Vacations

Everyone from Who is going to Where
To see what it is the people do over there.
Everyone from Where is going to Who
Everyone, except quite a few.
The people from What are going to Which
In which most of the people are rich
What attracts people to What, I don't know
The only way to find out is to go-
To What!

The Hobbit Tree

Feelings

Soft, doe-eyed, gentle-
Confused and hurt and torn-
Caught in a trap of tradition
That pulls and twists you
Night and Morn.
Making you question
Your values, your satisfactions
The love that you've found
And the care
Is anything really wrong
With these wonderful feelings
You share?

Blue Lake

Pondering

Don't push, don't prod,
Don't reach for the phone.
Some things are better
Left to sort out on their own.
I guess he needs security
He really wants you back.
He can't see how he ever
Got off on the wrong track.
I believe he really loves you
And he's such a wonderful guy
I wonder if you'd make it
If you gave it another try
He's a warm-hearted, people person
Kind and gentle, bold and shy.

Grace's Garden

You

I love you, really love you,
I care whether you live or die.
So, I've gone away to give you
Space to grow, to achieve, to try.
When I come back I hope
You've found a little more of yourself
I want to see you busy
Not sitting on a shelf
You've got such possibilities
Potential, talent and more.
You can never tell
What life holds in store.
I want to see you happy
Doing what's good for you.
I want you to make your own decisions,
To yourself be true.
Get out and share your talents
The world is waiting for you. Yes, YOU

Duelling Dragons

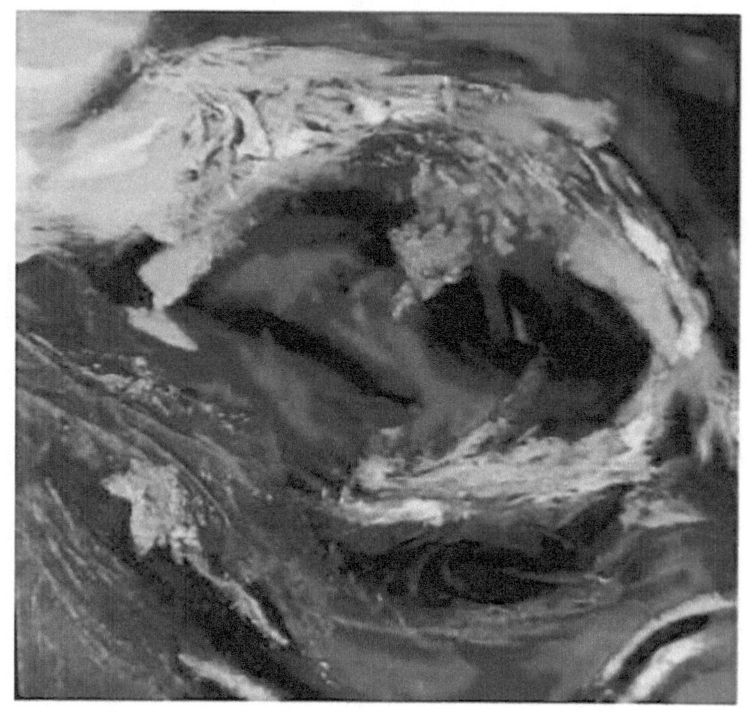

Control

Look carefully at your life and see
See what you really need—
A sense of control
Of power to solve life's crises
Of strength-pure, physical strength.
See what you really want- Love, unconditional and yielding
Definitely dependent love
Needing you, needing it. See why you live For others, for
their approval
BUT mostly for yourself
For your pleasures, for tomorrow. See how you live-
Narrowly, cautiously, afraid of the risk
Of trusting others
Of being let down. Afraid of life.
Look carefully at your life. Is this you?

Heron Haven

This Vehicle

My body, the vehicle of my life force
Carries me onward
Turning every which way—
Sometimes to the left, the logical side.
Often the brakes need adjusting
As I rush pell-mell toward life.
I need something to slow me down.
At times, the oil must be changed-
The exercise necessary for
flexibility and a long life
Must be done.
This vehicle needs a protective coating
To keep the skin supple and moist.
It requires high octane fuel-unleaded-
Special nutrition for top performance.
The windows need cleaning of anything
That obscures the vision of a full life.
Others watch the signals for direction
And mood change.
There is no cruise control on this model
Sometimes I proceed too quickly,
sometimes too slow.
Because this model has a short
wheelbase and front-wheel drive
It handles the curves life throws at it
And navigates through snowstorm
after snowstorm.
This vehicle, like any other good possession
Must be carefully maintained.

Aurora

Flying

Flying In my mind
Over the ocean
Over the ice flows
Over the volcanic field
Observing life from a distance
Able to see relationships and patterns
Fascinated by the rhythm and flow
Understanding, relating
The rounded, perfect cones of possible volcanoes
With the larger cones of dormant volcanoes
Of seeing lava flows
Pouring onto the surface of the earth
Lava flows cooked in some underground cauldron
Pouring forth when the cauldron
Can contain them no more.

Forest Monarch

Eventually

Believe the weather will get better,
It usually does,
Eventually.
Believe life will get better
It usually does
Eventually.
Believe your friends will understand you,
They usually do,
Eventually.
Try to get physically fit
You can
Eventually.
Try to live life well
You will
Eventually.
Try to see the positive side
You will
Eventually.
Try to find your niche in life
You will Eventually.

November

Why We Weep

Cry tears of release, of freedom from pain
Weep for joys forgotten, for chances long past.
Cleanse the aches from your body, your soul
Live through your fears
To see a fresh scrubbed tomorrow.
Weep and be comforted as others weep with you.
Weep for inaction, lack of
understanding, lack of love.
Weep because what we had was good.
It had its quiet pleasures
But that is gone...
Life became hollow, boring and dull.
That is why we weep.

Through the Century

Parents Concern

Where are you going?
And where have you been?
What time are you leaving?
What time do you get in?
Will you go by this way?
Can you bring me that?
What kind of clothes do you need?
Will you rent a flat?
These questions and more
Show a parent's concern.
They know we all have
So much more to learn.

Red Rock Canyon

Marriages

You love me, you hate me,
You really don't care.
Who ever said marriages were wash and wear.
This one is full of wrinkles
Its had the odd tear
It's been mended and mended
But it's not beyond repair.
It's a natural fabric
Comfortable but not easy care.
You need to fuss a bit, fume a bit
Adjust, alter and change.
You're not the person I married.
Wow, did you change!
I'm not sure I like it—
But it's really not bad
On one side, I hate it
On the other, I'm glad.
Why do you bug me?
What's wrong with you?
Settle down-you're a clown
No, I'm really not fair
But life's never boring
With two of us there.
Why do you need me?
Why do I need you?
Do we really help
One another?
I get in such a stew!

10:30pm

You Can

You can, you can,
You really can!
Do it yourself
Believe and plan.
Don't be afraid,
Don't hesitate
Get out,
Get on with life
Before it's too late.
You know what you want
You can see it so plain.
If you just dream
It will all be in vain.
Picture it in detail
See the satisfaction and the joy.
Don't miss the challenge
Life's not a toy.
Create, create, communicate.
Mix and mingle
Go explore
Ideas come often on life's busy shore.
Keep yourself flexible
Bend and twist
Things are humorous
When seen like this.
From this angle
From that angle
From up and from down.
Flex, curl,
Give it a whirl
You can, you can, you really CAN!

Blackbird

The Rubble

Climbing over the rubble of my life
Feeling the jagged rocks tear at me.
Some rocks worn smooth with time
Present themselves as wise choices
For rebuilding, recycling this life
Starting anew.
What changes will be made?
Not my friends—
They really know me-but, is that true? I
'm a strange combination
At times, too open-
At times, so well camouflaged
That even those I love haven't a clue.
Where does the agony come from?
The tears, the joy?
The struggle, the re-ordering?
Will the final product stand the test of time?
God, why am I so hard on me?
When will I ever learn-to just be?
I'm alone, so the tears can just roll down my face
Those few that I could share this with
I don't want to burden.
Some of the twisted girders will
have to be replaced
But there's a window that survived!
The stained glass in it I always did prize.
Now I can see what's salvageable
And what's not.
I'd better redesign on a more suitable plot.
I need something that is open,
that's warm, that's free.
I need space for some clutter,
Some books, the odd tree.
And room for someone who may come, go, or stay.
There may be some times I still
need to get far, far away.
There needs to be a place to study,
To think, to work, to play—
A little color,
Some memories to brighten a dull day.
It's strange the things that I cling to
What I discard, what I keep.

On the Move

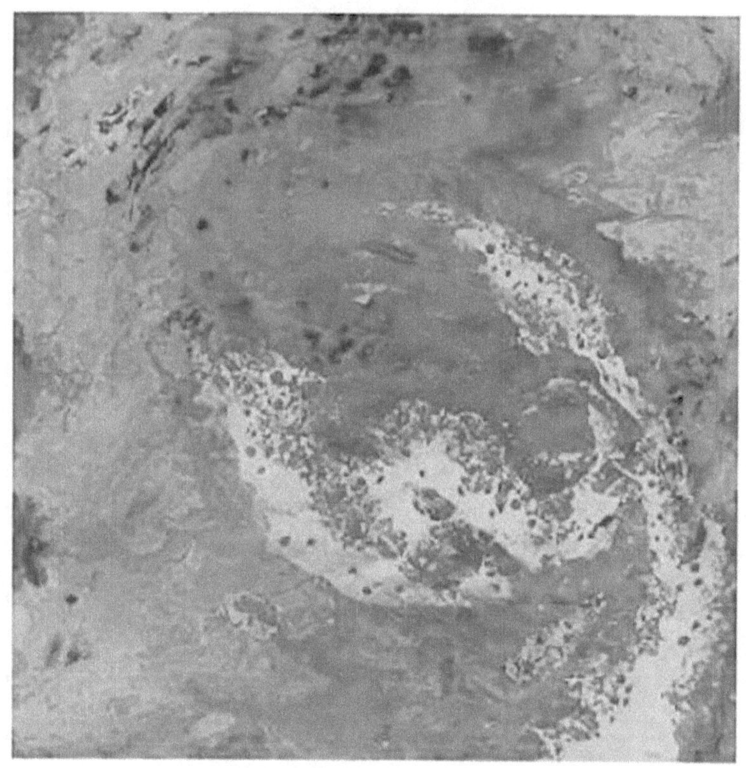

The Eternal Plan

Do you remember me after Marcie died?
Where did I ever get this foolish pride?
My grief was so private,
I just couldn't share it.
It was a strange thing to feel I
had the responsibility
to help others to bear it.
I used to cry when I was alone.
When no one else was even at home.
Maybe that was my way to atone
But I never really felt guilty-just so alone.
I loved her a lot.
What searching you go through
Trying to decide what you should feel
What is for now, what for later—
What is really real
How dare one question the Eternal Plan
Or judge the value of a short life span.
Some of us live like there's no tomorrow
No future joy, no future sorrow.
Who's to say what is best
Or who passes or fails the final test?

Sassy Sunflowers

Let Go

Let go! Relax! Enjoy!
Today has possibilities
A passing smile or wave
A phone call from a friend
A letter bringing news of someone at earth's end.
Today brings its new challenges
Other avenues to explore
It brings a time for accomplishment
A time for pleasures shared.
It may bring sorrows But we will handle those
Let go-be free of the future and
especially free of the past.
Don't let old memories haunt you
Free yourself at last.
They are over and done with.
Let go-tomorrow will take care of itself
The past and future need put on a shelf.
Feel the cold, the warmth, the joy-
Each minute is like a new toy
Let go! Relax! Enjoy!

Winter Birches

Tensions

I am tired of this tension,
This lack of understanding
And the tightness-
The resistance that drives it home.
I am weary of trying to think, to sort, to plan—
And yet, I feel I must.
It is my own whims I distrust.
I want to be me-to be free.
What will happen?
Wait and see.
Like others, I really don't understand me.

Madrone

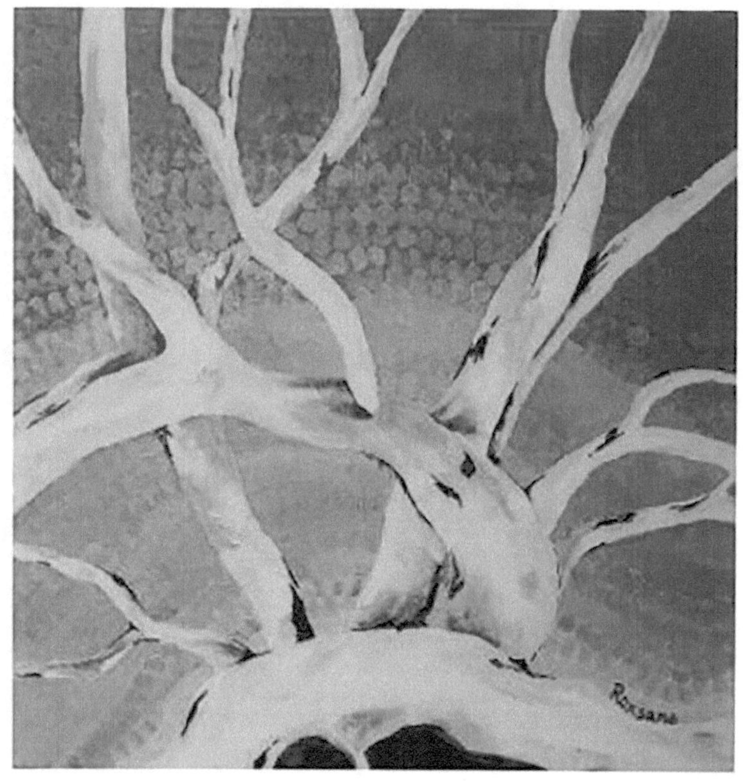

Stopped

There is a numbness to my life, A
frozen, timeless journey—
Going nowhere, doing nothing-stopped.
There is a great hollow ache
Echoing and re-echoing throughout
the caverns of my being.
There is an emptiness, a hollowness,
a numbness in my heart.
No feeling, no joy-only vast inner space-
An unfathomable, endless inner ocean
With tides of longing and despair.
I had a husband but no love
I had a child but it left home
I had reasons for life but they are gone.

Sea Pearls

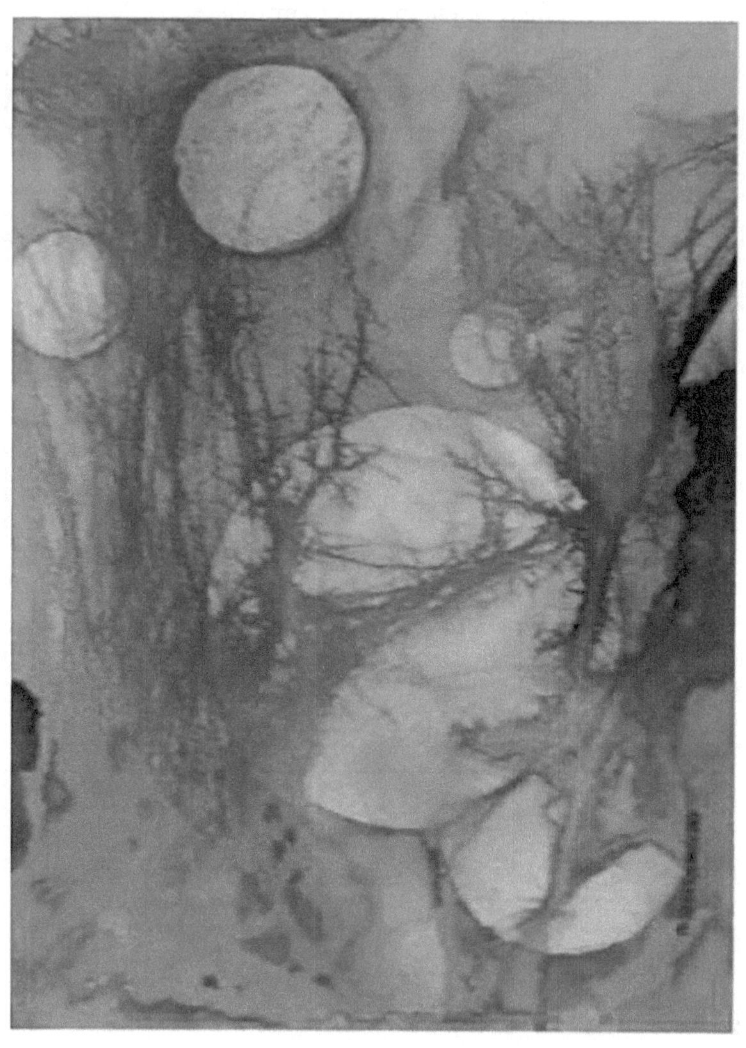

Why?

In some of my worst nightmares
I am alone, caught in a trap
I could have avoided if I hadn't been frozen,
unable to communicate, unable to move
To make decisions and to follow them through.
In some of my best dreams
I am busy, with friends, solving
problems, facing challenges—
Exploring new areas, helping and
understanding the world.

Bubble Wrap

How much more of my life can I avoid,
Encase in plastic, put on a shelf
and store forever—
To be opened when I least expect it
by some uninvited guest.

Arbutus Ridge

The Rebel

She must not resist life.
That would be totally wrong.
Resisting made life difficult.
There was only one thing to do
And that was to let go.
All her life she had resisted.
Resisting the trap of a strangling love
Resisting the tight narrow life styles
Forced on one by society and friends
Even the weather she resisted-
Its cold, chill fingers in the winter
And its searing, shriveling summer heat.
She did not accept life as it came.
She resisted giving in to its great pleasures
Almost as much as she resisted its pain.
She fought organization, exercise and direction.
Her whole life seemed dedicated
to a resistance of the
standard, the usual, the norm. She was a rebel.
This tight resistance had to go, go.
Could she never relax, unwind, accept?
Could she never?

Angles

Keep Trying

I've tried
And I've succeeded
And I can't be all that wrong
Have faith, have courage
Echoing and re-echoing throughout
the caverns of my being.
There is an emptiness, a hollowness, a numbness in my heart.
No feeling, no joy-only vast inner space- An unfathomable,
endless inner ocean With tides of longing and despair.
I had a husband but no love
I had a child but it left home
I had reasons for life but they are gone.
Friendly support can make you strong.
Some doubt you, some are jealous
Some really can't quite figure out you.
A little vision, A strong commitment
Occasional success can make you shout.
A crazy idea, A simple sharing,
A lot grows out of simply caring.
Reach out, Lend a hand-
Your idea may improve this community, this land.

Lush

Fireflies

Fireflies skimming over the lawn
Do they really flit from dusk to dawn?
Fireflies are very much like a smile
They light up their surroundings
for a short while.
Truly, they are much more beautiful than bees
Fireflies bring joy to one's heart
From the world of nature of which we are a part-
Fireflies send signals about in the dark,
Here and there all over the park.
Sheets of lightning brighten the sky
Hurry fireflies, Hurry by.

Presence

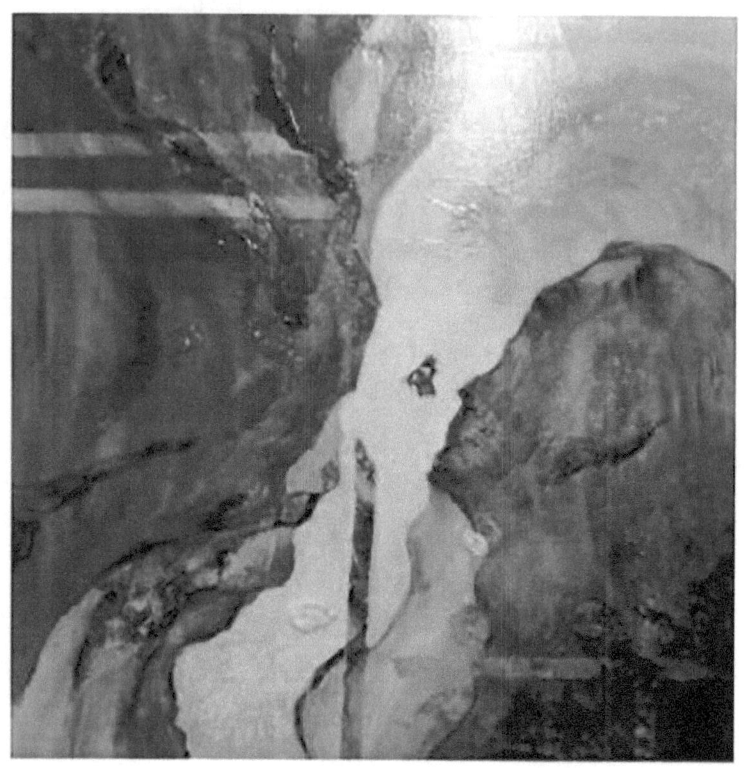

Courage

Courage when your back is to the wall
Courage when you think you're going to fall
Courage when you have to fight the fire
Courage when there's others to inspire
Courage when the way is all uphill
Courage when the enemy is there still
Courage when you feel the intense pain
Courage so you can go on again, again.
Courage that's what life is all about
Courage you can hear the others shout—
COURAGE

Where Dreams Begin

At Our Cabana

Between the old Japanese woman
And the young Mexican girl
Developed a friendship
As lustrous as a pearl.
They didn't know each other's language
But their souls cried out with joy.
The depth of their caring
The depth of their love
Provided a shower of blessings
That fell from above.

Coquitlam River

Life is full of wonder
The sun, the cold, the birds, the bees,
A child fascinated by a bug in the weeds.
Remember you have a lot to give
Things unique, all your own.
Your warmth, Your kindness,
Your love.

About the Athor

Roxsane was born and raised in the Greater Vancouver area. She became an international educator teaching high school and marketing for the district in Korea, Taiwan, Hong Kong, Japan, and Mexico. Wherever she travels she soaks up local colour, customs and cultural influences.

These cross-cultural experiences blend with her lively imagination, her creativity, and her love of the out-doors to provide an endless variety of subjects for her art work. Now, she lives in Burnaby.

One afternoon in Japan, in 1984, she took a class in Chigiri-e-a Japanese torn paper collage technique. This opened her creative channels. Now, she enjoys the variety of paper-the feel of it. It can be sturdy or fragile, bright or hazy, fibrous or sheer-gauzy. She loves it all.

Recently, Roxsane has experimented with the exuberance of acrylics using playful, audacious colour. Combining acrylics and paper, she creates mixed media pieces that tell stories. As president of the Burnaby Artists Guild, she has helped with the creation and completion of mosaic murals for the Tommy Douglas Library, the BC Children's Hospital, and two for the Burnaby General Hospital. Roxsane studied Applied Arts at Capilano College in the late 1970s, placing on the Dean's List. She has also taken several week-long workshops with well-known artists. She believes in lifelong learning. Her works are collected locally, nationally, and internationally. Roxsane is an energetic, hardworking, compulsive seventy-seven-year-old. She has caring, community-oriented siblings, two wonderful daughters, and five grandchildren.

Her wide circle of friends is scattered all over the globe, and at home she has a wonderful man named Bill who makes her life complete. Roxsane's early life was challenging but she completed her teacher's train- ing at UBC, taught in a one room school on Harrison Lake and married George Dheilly. Together they raised three beautiful daughters. The youngest, Marcia, died of a brain tumor in 1981. Their marriage fell apart in 1983-1984. Needing to find more meaning in her life, after the girls left home, she decided to go back to University to complete her Bachelor of Education, and get back to the most mean-ingful career she could find-teaching at the high school level. Since then, she has worked in Mexico for the World Association of Girl Guides and Girl Scouts, trav- eled extensively and taught International Students and immigrants before retiring and becoming a capable artist and author. "In my travels and through life, every time I enter a place of worship that I have never entered before, I ask—as I was taught to—to be given understanding or wisdom. They are gifts we all need. The content of my poems reflects what I have learned." - Roxsane Tiernan

End